Your Start-Up Starts Now!
A Guide to Entrepreneurship

What Is Social Entrepreneurship?

Margaret Hoogeveen

Crabtree Publishing Company
www.crabtreebooks.com

Author: Margaret Hoogeveen

Series research and development: Reagan Miller

Editor: Renata M. Brunner Jass, Kathy Middleton

Proofreader: Kelly Stern

Editorial services: Clarity Content Services

Project coordinator and prepress technician: Tammy McGarr

Print coordinator: Katherine Berti

Series consultant: Rebecca Darling

Cover design: Margaret Amy Salter

Design: David Montle

Photo Research: Linda Tanaka

Photo Credits:

Cover: All images from Shutterstock
Title page: Rawpixel.com/Shutterstock; p3 top Photo courtesy of Essmart, Courtesy of Liz Forkin Bohannon/Sseko Design, Tammy Tibbetts/She's the First; pp4-5 Dominic Chan/The Canadian Press; p6 top Library of Congress, Peter Mah/iStock, Public Domain/USA; p7 Alexander Davidyuk/Shutterstock; p8 CJM Grafx/Shutterstock; p9 Monkey Business Images/Shutterstock; p10 top Al Burafi/AP Photo/The Canadian Press, pp10-11 Photo courtesy of Toms; p12 National Library of Medicine, inset CCL/FormerBBC; p13 Courtesy of Duke University; p14 Yuri Cortez/AFP/Getty Images; p15 Dominic Chan/The Canadian Press; p16 Courtesy of Educate Girls; p17 Courtesy of Tariq Fancy; p18 CCL/Gregor Rohrig; p19 Courtesy of Ushahidi; pp20-21 Tatiana Kolesnik/Shutterstock; p22 Photo courtesy of Essmart; p24 NakarinZ/Shutterstock; p25 Lightkeeper/Dreamstime; p26 Photo courtesy of Essmart; p27 Photo courtesy of X-Runner; p28 Dean Drobot/Shutterstock; p29 Denphumi/Shutterstock; p31 Courtesy of Liz Forkin Bohannon/Sseko Design; p33 Brian Kelly/Empowerment Plan; p34 Bridget Hilton/LSTN Sound Co.; p35 Tammy Tibbetts/She's the First; p36 Courtesy of ONOIR; p37 Globe and Mail/The Canadian Press; p38 Simon Poon/Shutterstock; p39 paulaphoto/Shutterstock; p41 g-stockstudio/Shutterstock; p42 Courtesy of Yash Gupta; p43 beornbjorn/Shutterstock.

t=Top, bl=Bottom Left, br=Bottom Right

Library and Archives Canada Cataloguing in Publication

Hoovegen, Margaret, author
    What is social entrepreneurship? / Margaret Hoovegen.

(Your start-up starts now! a guide to entrepreneurship)
Includes bibliographical references and index.
Issued in print and electronic formats.
ISBN 978-0-7787-2757-6 (hardback).--
ISBN 978-0-7787-2765-1 (paperback).--
ISBN 978-1-4271-1823-3 (html)

        1. Social entrepreneurship--Juvenile literature. 2. Social responsibility of business--Juvenile literature. I. Title.

HD60.H667 2016   j658.4'08   C2016-903415-1
                                                                          C2016-903416-X

Library of Congress Cataloging-in-Publication Data

Names: Hoovegen, Margaret, author.
Title: What is social entrepreneurship? / Margaret Hoovegen.
Description: New York : Crabtree Publishing, [2017] |
    Series: Your start-up starts now! A guide to entrepreneurship |
    Includes bibliographical references and index.
Identifiers: LCCN 2016026653 (print) | LCCN 2016038423 (ebook) |
    ISBN 9780778727576 (reinforced library binding) |
    ISBN 9780778727651 (pbk.) |
    ISBN 9781427118233 (Electronic HTML)
Subjects: LCSH: Social entrepreneurship--Juvenile literature.
Classification: LCC HD60 .H667 2017 (print) | LCC HD60 (ebook) |
    DDC 658.4/08--dc23
LC record available at https://lccn.loc.gov/2016026653

Crabtree Publishing Company
www.crabtreebooks.com   1-800-387-7650

Printed in Canada/102016/IH20160811

Published in Canada
Crabtree Publishing
616 Welland Ave.
St. Catharines, Ontario
L2M 5V6

Published in the United States
Crabtree Publishing
PMB 59051
350 Fifth Avenue, 59th Floor
New York, New York 10118

Published in the United Kingdom
Crabtree Publishing
Maritime House
Basin Road North, Hove
BN41 1WR

Published in Australia
Crabtree Publishing
3 Charles Street
Coburg North
VIC, 3058

Contents

Doing Things Differently

Why do you buy stuff? Do things like bracelets, basketballs, or earbuds make your life more comfortable or more fun? Perhaps they do. If you choose carefully, though, your purchases can do something else, too: they can help change the world.

Craig and Marc Kielburger energize the crowd at a WE Day event. They hold these events to inspire youth to work for positive change in the world.

Seeking a New Way of Doing Things

In 2008, Canadian brothers Craig and Marc Kielburger were running a **charity**. It was called Free the Children (now called WE Charity). Through this charity, the brothers were doing remarkable things. They were helping children escape slavery and go to school. The problem was that the Kielburger brothers needed more money to do this work. So they founded ME to WE.

ME to WE is an enterprise, which is a business organization. Many enterprises sell things to help them meet a single goal: to make money. ME to WE sells a variety of things to meet a different goal: to change the world. That's why it gives half of all its **profits** to WE Charity (formerly Free the Children) and invests the other half back into the enterprise.

ME to WE is just one of many enterprises trying to find ways to change the world. The next time you're feeling torn between buying something for yourself and supporting a good cause, stop and think. Remember that you can do both at the same time!

ME to WE is an example of **social entrepreneurship**. A social enterprise may help people directly, or it may raise funds to donate to other groups. It may make a profit for its owners or **investors**. In all cases, the main goal of social entrepreneurship is to address a social problem.

1 Social Entrepreneurship

Have you ever run a lemonade stand? You would have planned it out, bought your supplies, and made it happen. That would make you an **entrepreneur**. An entrepreneur is someone who plans, starts, and runs a new enterprise that provides **goods** or **services**.

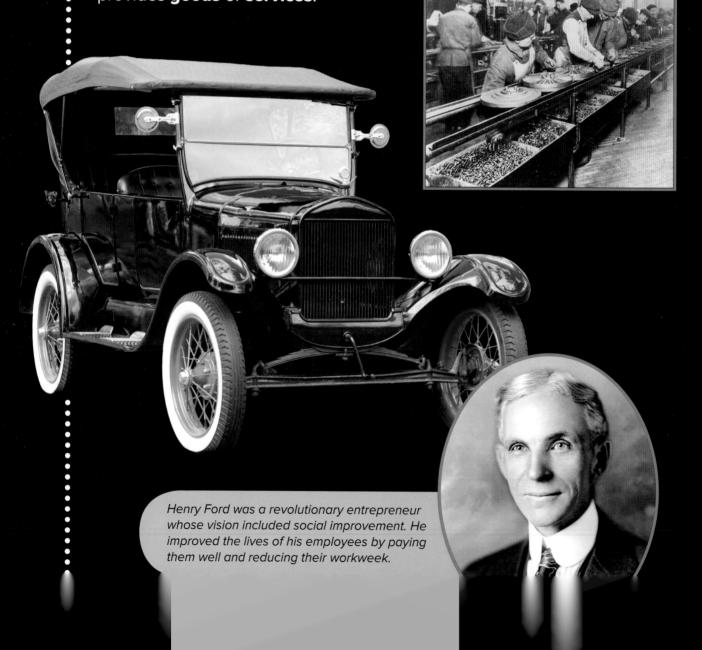

Henry Ford was a revolutionary entrepreneur whose vision included social improvement. He improved the lives of his employees by paying them well and reducing their workweek.

Groundbreaking Entrepreneurs

Some entrepreneurs do things that change people's lives. One famous American entrepreneur was Henry Ford. In 1908, his company introduced the Model T automobile. It was affordable and simple to drive. In 1914, Ford began producing this car on a moving **assembly line**. This had never been done before. The new approach made production easy and kept costs low. The Model T's low price allowed many more people in North America to buy a car for the first time.

More importantly, Ford's assembly line changed the way many things were made. Using an assembly line to make automobiles meant that more cars could be built in less time. The cars could still be good quality but cost less. Workers had shorter workdays, yet made good money. Ford's success inspired business owners worldwide to use assembly lines in all kinds of industries. Today, everything from toasters to party hats are made using assembly lines.

Forms of Entrepreneurship

All entrepreneurs follow a passion. They tend to be good at noticing a problem or need, and then finding a solution for it. Traditionally, entrepreneurs have focused on keeping customers and making a profit. In recent years, people have begun to use business skills to develop new kinds of enterprises.

In an automobile assembly line, cars move through a series of stations. At each station, a worker installs the same part on every car.

Many entrepreneurs have found business opportunities providing goods and services over the Internet. The main goal of **digital entrepreneurship** is the same as that of most businesses: to make money.

Most businesses measure their success by whether they make a profit. Suppose you sold a lot of lemonade at your lemonade stand. You would probably make a profit, so your business would be considered a success!

Social and **environmental entrepreneurship** are different. Such enterprises may generate a profit, but that is not their main goal. Environmental entrepreneurs are passionate about having a positive impact on environmental issues. The main goal of social entrepreneurs is to have a positive effect on people's lives.

Making Social Change Happen

This book is about social entrepreneurship. Social entrepreneurs are good at finding clever solutions to address social problems such as child labor, poverty, lack of **sanitation**, hunger, **racism**, or low **literacy**. Social problems around the world are almost too many to count. All social entrepreneurs have one thing in common: they share a passion to help improve the lives of others.

What message might this girl be sending to her customers by her unique spelling of the word "lemonade" on her sign?

Not Just About the Money

Like all entrepreneurs, social entrepreneurs plan and run new enterprises. They provide goods or services, and they must be financially responsible. Unlike other enterprises, a social enterprise is only successful if it makes social change. Suppose you want to help families who can't afford to buy food. If you set up a lemonade stand to raise money and donated half of your profits to a local food bank, that would make you a successful social entrepreneur!

What qualities would you use to inspire your team to help you change the world?

Qualities of a Social Entrepreneur

All entrepreneurs are problem solvers driven by a sense of purpose. Social entrepreneurs have the action-oriented nature of an entrepreneur as well as a powerful sense of social responsibility.

Nearly every entrepreneur has worked hard to develop the qualities he or she needed to succeed. Many social entrepreneurs remember becoming concerned with social issues when they were young. They learned skills that would help them become successful social entrepreneurs. That means you can, too.

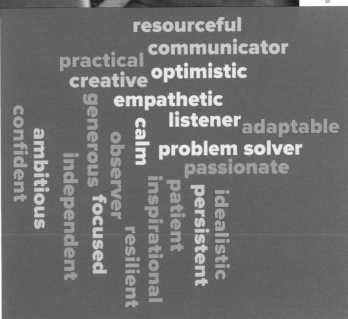

resourceful
communicator
practical optimistic
creative
empathetic
listener adaptable
problem solver
passionate
idealistic
persistent
patient
inspirational
calm
observer
resilient
generous focused
independent
ambitious
confident

Which of these qualities would most help a social entrepreneur?

One Pair of Shoes at a Time

In the photo above, the shoes are being handed out in a community. In TOMS's first "Shoe Drop," 10,000 pairs of shoes were distributed in schools and small communities in Argentina. In the photo to the right, Blake Mycoskie delivers TOMS shoes.

Social enterprises can take many forms. Some are charities that depend on **donations**. Others, like TOMS Shoes, are businesses that make a profit. TOMS is a social enterprise because the purpose of the company is social change.

At the age of 29, Blake Mycoskie was running his fourth business. It was an online driver education course for teens.

Mycoskie needed a break, so he traveled to Argentina. There, he noticed people wearing a cool-looking shoe called an *alpargata*. He also noticed many barefoot children whose families were too poor to buy shoes. Mycoskie got two ideas on that trip. He wanted to make *alpargata* shoes to sell in the United States. He also wanted to do something to help all those kids.

Mycoskie started TOMS Shoes. It makes a profit while creating social change at the same time. Mycoskie made a commitment at the very beginning: for every pair of shoes that he sold, he would give a pair to a child who needed them. This is now known as a One-for-One business model. TOMS Shoes became very popular. The story interested people. They were excited to buy a pair of shoes, knowing that their purchase could also make someone else's life a little better.

Mycoskie and his small team sold an amazing 10,000 pairs of shoes in their first six months of business in 2006. As of 2016, TOMS had given away more than 50 million pairs of shoes on five continents. Now *that's* making a difference!

> ❝All at once, [TOMS] made a living for me and everyone who worked at TOMS, it brought me closer to the people and places I loved, and it offered me a way to contribute something to people in need.❞
>
> – Blake Mycoskie, Founder and Chief Shoe Giver, TOMS Shoes

These three girls have shoes because three people in other countries bought shoes for themselves from TOMS.

Blake Mycoskie's One-for-One Business Model		
	Sell one . . .	Provide one . . .
TOMS Shoes	pair of shoes	pair of shoes to a child who has none
TOMS Eyewear	pair of glasses	pair of glasses to a child who needs them
TOMS Roasting Co.	bag of coffee	week's worth of clean water to a person in need

Mycoskie has applied his One-for-One business model to several businesses.

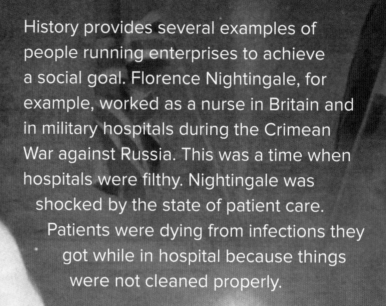

History provides several examples of people running enterprises to achieve a social goal. Florence Nightingale, for example, worked as a nurse in Britain and in military hospitals during the Crimean War against Russia. This was a time when hospitals were filthy. Nightingale was shocked by the state of patient care. Patients were dying from infections they got while in hospital because things were not cleaned properly.

Florence Nightingale was idealized by a whole generation. In this 1891 painting, artist Henrietta Rae portrays the famous nurse tending to wounded soldiers.

The British nurse Florence Nightingale is shown at center, surrounded by students. She was an early advocate for the use of medical statistics to improve health care.

In response, in 1860, Nightingale started the world's first nursing school, and began teaching new methods of nursing. Nightingale's most important change to nursing was to formally include training for nurses in proper sanitation. Her goals in setting up the school were to revolutionize health care and to save lives, especially those of soldiers and poor people.

The Social Entrepreneur: A New Idea

Many people like Nightingale have run individual businesses with social goals. The idea of social entrepreneurship, however, has been studied for only a few decades. A professor named J. Gregory Dees at Duke University in North Carolina was a pioneer in teaching modern social entrepreneurship. He saw something that other people did not: that the practices of entrepreneurship could be used to solve major world problems. He knew this was an effective way to address poverty, hunger, pollution, and other issues. Dees inspired people to develop social enterprises that would change the world.

Dees described social entrepreneurs as sharing common characteristics and behaviors:

- They adopt a mission to achieve a social goal, not just an economic goal.
- They recognize opportunities to help them achieve their goals.
- They continually create, adapt, and learn.
- They act boldly.
- They have a sense of social responsibility.

An Explosion of Rethinking

These days, everyone is talking about social entrepreneurship. People wonder if it can really work. Can we use the tools and techniques of entrepreneurs to change the world?

More and more people want to give social entrepreneurship a try. Universities now offer courses about how to set up a social enterprise. Networking organizations have formed so that social entrepreneurs can share their ideas. Some organizations give money to new social enterprises to help them get started. Social entrepreneurship has taken the world by storm.

Professor J. Gregory Dees inspired a generation of social entrepreneurs.

Turning Banking on Its Head

One of the best known social enterprises began in Bangladesh. In the 1970s, most people in Bangladesh were extremely poor. Wealthier nations were sending money to the country in the form of financial aid, to help with big development projects like bridges, highways, and railways. The money was not, however, helping people who were very poor.

Muhammad Yunus taught economics at a Bangladeshi university. He had an idea that would help people work their way out of poverty. His solution was to form a bank that would give out **microcredit**, or tiny **loans**. The loans were always small, maybe only $50 or $100. The loans were offered to people who needed a little money to start a small business.

Nolberta Melara of shows off one of the aprons she makes using a sewing machine that she purchased with microcredit.

Yunus called his bank Grameen Bank. *Grameen* means "village" in Bengali, the native language of Bangladesh. His idea caught on, especially among women. Very few Bengali women had ever been given a loan before. Most started small businesses and then paid back their loans. Some were able to expand their businesses and hire workers, improving life in their communities.

Grameen Bank is not a charity. It charges money for its services. By making money, the bank can grow, give more loans, and remain independent. It never needs to find funding from other sources.

How does microcredit actually work for an individual? Here is how it worked for Nolberta Melara:

How Microcredit Works

Microcredit Step	What Nolberta Melara Did
A person has a great idea but no money.	Nolberta Melara of El Salvador wanted to make aprons to sell in the marketplace. She did not have money to buy a sewing machine.
A microcredit bank loans money to the person.	A local microbusiness center loaned Melara $30, which she used to buy a sewing machine.
The person starts his or her own business.	Melara makes beautiful aprons, which she sells in markets across the country.
The person earns a better income.	Melara can now support her family financially.

Microcredit: Setting a Good Example

Yunus's microcredit bank was so successful in Bangladesh that other social entrepreneurs created similar loan-granting banks in other countries. Within a few years, the idea had spread like wildfire. Some enterprises failed, but many others succeeded. People admired Yunus for building an enterprise to solve a social problem. Grameen Bank's success inspired others to think of enterprises that they might use to solve different social problems.

In 2006, Muhammad Yunus and Grameen Bank received the Nobel Peace Prize. It made Yunus famous. He uses his fame to help social businesses address problems around the world.

Grameen Bank: Just the Facts

- Founded: 1976
- Loans granted by 2007: $6 billion
- Loan recipients by 2007: 7 million in 73,000 Bangladeshi villages
- Percentage of recipients who are women: 97
- Number of microcredit programs inspired by Grameen worldwide by 2005: 3,100

3 Why They Do It

Social entrepreneurs are asked again and again why they do what they do. They usually give one of two types of responses:

- Some are concerned about the state of the world. They see an **injustice** and feel it must be fixed.

- Others have a personal reason. They feel a lack of meaning in their own lives.

By starting a social enterprise, social entrepreneurs can address both problems: they can build meaning in their own lives while working to fix an injustice.

Safeena Husain with a group of students

Tariq Fancy: Founder, The Rumie Initiative

Tariq Fancy has roots in many places. His parents moved from Kenya to Canada, where Fancy was born and raised. He later became a highly successful **investment** banker in the United States. However, Fancy felt like he was "living somebody else's dream." The money he earned was not making him happy. So he gave up his job and changed his life.

Fancy is now busy educating the world through Rumie, his social enterprise. Rumie makes a low-cost, low-energy tablet for children in developing countries. Most children in low-income areas do not have reliable access to the Internet, so every Rumie tablet is pre-loaded with plenty of useful, reliable, and free educational content. Any child with a Rumie tablet can learn, even if he or she doesn't go to school or have Internet access.

By 2015, Rumie was operating in seven countries and had sold 30,000 of its tablets. Fancy's goal is to supply enough tablets to educate the one billion children worldwide who cannot go to school.

Tariq Fancy with a Rumie tablet

Social entrepreneur Safeena Husain founded Educate Girls to address a social injustice in India. India has the lowest number of girls attending school than any other country in the world. Only one in 100 girls completes high school. Husain was determined to change that. She formed Team Balika, a group of young, educated women who visit remote villages. They go from door to door to find every girl not in class. They convince the families that school is good for the girls and their families. They help parents feel a sense of ownership of the school and get them involved. Team Balika also goes into classrooms to show how learning can be fun. Husain's project is working. So far, Educate Girls has enrolled more than 110,000 girls from 4,500 villages in 8,000 schools.

Changing the World

Ory Okolloh founded Ushahidi to help the people of Kenya protect themselves.

In early 2008, Kenya was a country in crisis. Within just a few months, 1,000 people had been killed in ethnic violence. Another 500,000 people were displaced, meaning they had been forced to move from their home areas. Ordinary people were getting very little information about the crisis. They did not know which neighborhoods were dangerous.

Ory Okolloh was part of an online community of technology experts in Kenya. When the violence began, she saw the need for Kenyans to have information-sharing technology. In response, she founded Ushahidi, an online mapping program. People can use it to post a report when they see an event in an ongoing crisis. The Ushahidi software puts the locations on an online map. Relief workers, activists, and other people can easily access the data. They can use it to communicate with each other and with those seeking to help victims. Today, Ushahidi is used in over 160 countries, helping people to stay informed about dangerous situations worldwide.

You make the call…

Social entrepreneurs often find a way to revolutionize, or completely change, how something is done. How are Safeena Husain, Tariq Fancy, and Ory Okolloh each doing that in their own way?

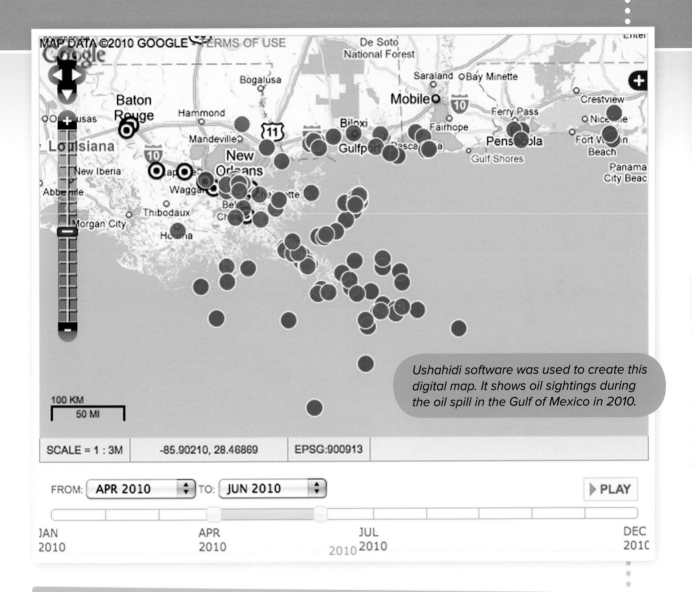

Ushahidi software was used to create this digital map. It shows oil sightings during the oil spill in the Gulf of Mexico in 2010.

❚❚[Some] people see and feel things that others don't. But you have to believe that everything is possible. If you believe it, those around you will believe it, too. **❚❚**

—Anita Roddick, Founder, The Body Shop, describing how entrepreneurs see things differently. The Body Shop dedicates its business to creating social and environmental change.

Let's Change the World

Social entrepreneurs share a passion—they all want to make the world a better place. At the same time, they are all different. Each is influenced by individual circumstances and values. Read what a few of them have to say about why they do what they do.

❝ There is something different in the air these days. . . . Increasingly, the quest for success is not the same as the quest for status and money. The definition has broadened to include contributing something to the world and living and working on one's own terms. ❞

– Blake Mycoskie, United States,
Founder and Chief Shoe Giver of TOMS Shoes

UNITED STATES

BRITAIN

❝ I want to work for a company that contributes to and is part of the community. I want something not just to invest in. I want something to believe in. ❞

– Anita Roddick, Britain,
Founder of The Body Shop

❝ When I started Teach For America, I wasn't trying to come up with an idea that would change the world. I was trying to solve a problem that was much closer to home: I was a senior in college and I had no idea what I was going to do with my life! ❞

– Wendy Kopp, United States,
Founder of Teach For America, which works to place good teachers in low-income neighborhood schools

> " I learned a lot sitting and talking with the women of [the village of] Jobra; I came to know about things which I had never imagined. I longed to do whatever I could to help them. "

— Muhammad Yunus, Bangladesh, Founder of Grameen Bank

> " As I served my cabbage to the guests and they thanked me for helping to feed them, I knew I could and I should do more to help. . . . My dream is that there are no hungry people. "

— Katie Stagliano, United States, Founder of Katie's Krops, which coordinates youth to grow vegetables for people in need

BANGLADESH

INDIA

> " Ten years later, I will be able to say, 'I saw [the] future happen.' And this is the most rewarding part of what I do. "

— Sharad Vivek Sagar, India, Founder of Dexterity Global, which works to bring educational opportunities to students in South Asia

?

You make the call...

People have different reasons for creating social enterprises. What reasons can you spot in the quotes on these two pages? Suppose that you wanted to start a social enterprise. What reasons would most inspire you?

Diana Jue and Jackie Stenson are two social entrepreneurs. They recognized a distribution problem: life-improving products were not getting to the people who needed them. Jue and Stenson teamed up to solve the problem.

Diana Jue (left) and Jackie Stenson (right), founders of Essmart

There are several steps that businesses and entrepreneurs follow to achieve a goal. On the following pages, walk through the steps that Jue and Stenson took as they built their enterprise, Essmart Global.

Identify a Problem

Entrepreneurs are good observers. They notice problems. They notice when solutions aren't working, and why. Americans Diana Jue and Jackie Stenson were both interested in many amazing new technologies designed to make life easier for people in rural, low-income areas. These items included a bicycle-powered phone charger, solar-powered lights, and a bacteria-killing water filter. Between 2008 and 2011, Jue traveled in India, and Stenson traveled in Africa. They both noticed that these life-improving products were not getting into the hands of the people they were made for.

Jue and Stenson learned that the two most common methods being used to distribute the life-improving products were not working. Charitable organizations gave products away, but they often ran out of money. Manufacturers tried to sell their products directly, but they made all the decisions about who could access them. Neither would fix an item if it broke.

Research the Market

After identifying an entrepreneurial opportunity, entrepreneurs do **market research**. They try to learn whether their product or service will satisfy people's needs and expectations.

Jue and Stenson's research revealed that every community in India has a little retail shop that local people trust. This provided a network of local sales outlets for them to sell to. Their entrepreneurial solution was to start a distribution company called Essmart Global in 2011. Essmart connects the manufacturers of life-improving products with the most trusted local shopkeepers in India.

Make a Business Plan

A **business plan** is a document detailing how an enterprise will achieve its goals. It has to answer questions about how the business will operate, who will do the work, and how much money will be needed for **start-up costs**.

Since most of the products they would sell were already available in India, Jue and Stenson would only be distributing inventory, not warehousing it. That made their business plan fairly simple. They would create an Essmart catalog featuring 66 different technologies produced by a variety of manufacturers. Essmart would send salespeople out with the catalog to the retail shops to get them to order Essmart Global products.

If Essmart grows, this hardware shop in Leh Ladakh, India, could soon sell Essmart products.

Find Start-Up Funding

Every enterprise has start-up costs, so entrepreneurs must find funding. Generally, there are four sources for funds: 1) you can use your own money; 2) you can get a bank loan, which you must repay with **interest**; 3) individuals or corporations may invest in your enterprise, for which they will expect a financial return; or 4) you may get donations from individuals or businesses, who will expect a social return, such as impact on a social problem.

Crowdfunding is another method for funding a new enterprise. Crowdfunding websites provide places for entrepreneurs to post a **pitch** for their ideas to a lot of people at once. The entrepreneur asks for tiny loans, donations, or investments. Contributors usually receive a product, service, or ownership share in return.

Some organizations support social entrepreneurship with **grants**. Essmart Global was awarded an IDEAS Venture Grant of $12,500 from the Massachusetts Institute of Technology. They also won the Dell Social Innovation Challenge in 2012, which awards the winner $50,000 and provides **mentoring**, or guidance, from experienced entrepreneurs.

Crowdfunding reduces risk. If a crowdfunded project fails, a lot of people lose just a little. If it succeeds, a lot of people win.

Hire Staff

Getting the right staff in place is critical to a new enterprise. The ideal employees are skilled people who are also passionate about the social goal of the enterprise. Jue and Stenson worked hard to find people passionate about improving the lives of others.

Run a Pilot Project

Many enterprises run a **pilot project**, or a test run. The business starts by operating in a small part of the market. The goal is to figure out what works and what doesn't. What do customers like? Is the idea practical? Positive results may attract more investors. Jue and Stenson ran a pilot project in 2012. Two shops in Pollachi, India, sold 17 technologies in one week. This success indicated their idea would work.

> ❚❚ A lot of the shop owners ... really were interested— not just because of the [money they could make]. They were saying things like, 'Oh, this could really improve our people's lives.' ❚❚
>
> – Diana Jue, Co-founder, Essmart Global

Reaching Customers

Market Your Product or Service

Before a business can make any sales, customers must know about its goods or services, and be inspired to make a purchase. **Marketing** is the promotion of a company and its product or service. Marketing includes advertising and building name recognition. Essmart designed a **logo**, which is a symbol of a company, and created shop displays. They also sent out catalogs to potential customers.

Serve Your Customers

Keeping customers happy is a key to business success. Businesses must supply good information and deliver their product or service on time. To provide their customers with good service, Essmart employees teach the shop owners how to use the products. They supply user manuals and fix or replace faulty items. This gives customers a reason to trust Essmart, as well as the shop owners they are buying from.

A logo helps customers recognize a company and its products or services.

Plan for Expansion

Most businesses want to grow. More sales mean bigger profits. Growth can also increase the company's social impact. Jue and Stenson want to expand Essmart Global so they can improve more people's lives. Their market research shows that there are about 14 million shops in India that could be potential Essmart customers!

Isabel Medem: CEO and Co-founder, x-runner Venture

Isabel Medem, a social entrepreneur from Germany, recognized a problem. Regular toilets only work with running water, but many low-income neighborhoods around the world do not have access to running water. People in these places must use pit latrines, which are simply holes dug in the ground. They are unsanitary and cause disease.

Medem had heard about a toilet that worked without using water. In 2010, she teamed up with Jessica Altenburger, an industrial designer from Switzerland, and created an business plan to address the problem. Their idea was to sell the waterless toilets along with a service to pick up the waste from the toilets. Medem's mother is from Peru. Ten million people in Peru do not have access to toilets. It was the perfect place to run their pilot project.

Medem and Altenburger found investors, who provided money for the company's start-up costs. They called the company x-runner. They hired local staff in Peru and started work. Isabel listens carefully to her customers, even the ones who stop using x-runner. She says, "It is incredibly important to be in tune with and analyze why someone is saying yes or no."

Isabel Medem sits on one of the waterless toilets that x-runner sells. Urine is directed underground. Feces are covered in sawdust. For a $13 fee, an x-runner team collects the waste once per week.

? You make the call...

The steps Isabel Medem and x-runner followed for starting and running their enterprise are outlined in this chapter. How could you use these steps to start a social enterprise that benefits a group in need in your community?

5

Finding the Right Balance

In legal terms, all enterprises can be defined as either **not-for-profit** or **for-profit**. A social enterprise can make a profit or not, but in order for an enterprise to be considered a social enterprise, it must have social change as its main goal. Social entrepreneurship can take many forms. A social enterprise can be big or small. It can buy, sell, or give away any kind of good or service.

Smithsonian Institute

Not-for-profit enterprises

tion Army

an Heart
ociation

Sierra Club

Save the
Children

WE Charity

Charities

Doctors Without Borders

Make–A–Wish
Foundation

TOMS
Shoes

Sseko
Designs

For-profit enterprises

Apple, Inc.

Microsoft

A charity is a form of not-for-profit enterprise.

For-Profit Enterprises

For-profit enterprises exist to make money for their owners and investors. They pay **taxes** on their profits. Any for-profit business can also have a positive social impact, for example, if it donates money to charities. Many for-profit enterprises include corporate social responsibility (CSR) in their business plan. CSR sets out ethical considerations to guide the company in its activities. For example, a company may make a commitment to operate in ways that are not harmful to the economy, the environment, or society.

Entrepreneurs can drive social change by making it the main purpose of a for-profit company. A business like TOMS Shoes (pages 10–11) makes money for its investors and owners. It is also a social enterprise because its main purpose is to provide free shoes to children in need.

Not-for-Profit Enterprises

Not-for-profit enterprises do not exist to make money for their owners or investors. All **revenue** must be used to pay salaries and **expenses** or to support the organization's social goal. Any extra revenue left over after expenses are paid must be put back into the organization. Not-for-profit enterprises do not pay taxes on their revenue.

Many not-for-profit enterprises are charities. Governments grant this special tax-free status to organizations that seek to relieve human suffering. Doctors Without Borders, for example, is a charity. All of its revenue helps bring medical care to people in disaster zones.

Return on Investment

Social entrepreneurs can get start-up money from either **donors** or investors. Both expect some form of benefit, called a **return on investment**.

Donors usually give money to not-for-profit social enterprises. They expect a social return on investment, or social impact. They want to help create social change.

Investors give money to for-profit social enterprises. They receive a share of the ownership. Most expect a financial return on investment, or a share of the profits. They also expect a social return on investment. The combination of social and financial return varies with different enterprises.

 Donors and investors want something to grow from their money: social change, profits, or both.

Keeping on Track

Noticing a Problem

In 2008, Liz Bohannon graduated from college. She got a good job but was unhappy. So she quit her job and went traveling instead. In Uganda she made friends with other young women. They were bright and talented high school graduates. In Uganda, all students must take a nine-month break between high school and college. During that time, they work and save their money for college. But jobs are scarce in Uganda. Many women cannot attend college because they cannot get a job first.

Finding a Solution

Bohannon decided to create a business that would provide jobs. She first tried a chicken farm, but that **venture** failed. Then she remembered sandals she had worn in college. Bohannon wondered if she could start a shoe factory in Uganda.

This was the beginning of Sseko Designs, which Bohannon founded with her husband, Ben. (The word "sseko" means *laughter* in Lugandan, the major language in Uganda.) The company employs Ugandan women who want to go to college. Sseko pays them a fair wage. Every month, half of each employee's salary goes into a savings account. At the end of nine months, a woman has enough to pay for her tuition. Sseko Designs achieves its social goal and also makes a profit. By 2016, Sseko had provided 71 young women with the opportunity to go to college.

Keeping the Goal in Mind

Entrepreneurs often face obstacles. For example, Liz and Ben Bohannon tried to convince potential investors to invest in Sseko Designs. The investors advised the Bohannons to have the sandals made cheaply in China, grow the company quickly, get rich, and then donate money to help women in Uganda.

If they had followed this advice, the Bohannons might have had an easier time getting investors. But they stuck with their plan. They believe their business will make the world a better place.

> ❚❚ The truth is, there are very few things you can't overcome! Every win and every loss is creating a larger [story]. Don't freak out about the individual highs and lows—stay focused on your long-term vision. ❚❚
>
> – Liz Forkin Bohannon, Co-Founder, Sseko Designs

Liz Bohannon believes that business is about more than getting rich. She believes that businesses can make a profit and make a difference at the same time.

? You make the call...

You have started an enterprise making phone cases. Your goal is to employ people with differing physical abilities and pay them a fair wage. A potential investor offers to give you the money you need to start operations, on one condition: he will not pay to make your production facility wheelchair-accessible. He thinks it is an unnecessary cost. How do you respond? Explain your thinking.

6

Strategies for Social Change

Passion drives all entrepreneurs, and creativity is their key to finding solutions. Social entrepreneurs also use at least one of the three strategies below to achieve their goals.

Spending Money

Employing People

Providing Goods and Services

The Empowerment Plan

The Empowerment Plan is a social enterprise based in Detroit, Michigan. Its goal is to "help build a better life for those that have become trapped in the cycle of homelessness." The enterprise makes a winter coat that converts into a sleeping bag. The Empowerment Plan uses all three strategies of the social entrepreneur.

Spending money. As a not-for-profit enterprise, The Empowerment Plan does not exist to create a financial return for its founder, Veronika Scott, or its main supporter, Carhartt Inc. Instead, all investments and donations help homeless people. Donors provide money to buy coats, sewing machines, and even daycare for the employees.

Employing people. All people sewing for The Empowerment Plan are or have been homeless. The enterprise trains them and pays them a fair wage. This enables them to support themselves and their children, and to find housing.

Providing goods and services. Keeping warm in winter can be a huge challenge for people without a place to stay. The items that Scott's enterprise produces directly help to improve people's lives.

Veronika Scott:
Founder, The Empowerment Plan

Veronika Scott founded The Empowerment Plan while studying design in her hometown of Detroit. She was assigned to design a product that would help address a local problem.

Scott focused on homelessness. To develop a good solution, Scott had to consult the people she wanted to serve. So she spoke to a group of homeless women. At first, she was nervous and didn't know what to say. She finally blurted out, "I'm broke and living with my grandparents, and I really need your help with my class project!"

After months of talking with people, Scott finally had an idea: the sleeping-bag coat. But she didn't know how to sew! Her mother helped her, using a home sewing machine. Afterward, Scott had her first prototype, or test model, of her product. By 2016, The Empowerment Plan was giving away coats in 29 states and three Canadian provinces.

Veronika Scott (left) working with an employee at The Empowerment Plan. Women who work here can soon afford a home for themselves.

Spending Money

Nearly all social enterprises spend money in order to achieve their social goals. In the example of The Empowerment Plan, the company spends money from donations to help homeless people.

Spending Sales Revenue

For some social enterprises, neither their product nor their power to employ people directly addresses the social problem they aim to help. Instead, they use their profits to achieve social improvement.

Bridget Hilton has a for-profit company named LSTN Headphones. This business makes high-quality headphones. Its goal is to "change lives through the power of music." Specifically, it addresses the social problem of hearing loss. The headphones themselves do not directly address hearing loss. However, the company uses part of the profits from the sales of its headphones to buy hearing aids for people who cannot afford them. In its first three years of business, LSTN helped 20,000 people with hearing loss in the United States, Peru, Indonesia, Kenya, Uganda, China, and Sri Lanka.

Bridget Hilton poses with a set of the high-end headphones her company produces.

Spending Donations

Not every social enterprise generates revenue. Some use the skills and the strategies of entrepreneurship to generate donations. Donations, like profits, can be used to address a social problem.

Tammy Tibbets and Christen Brandt co-founded the not-for-profit enterprise She's the First in 2009. She's the First has just a few employees, makes no product, and generates no sales revenue. Instead, it generates donations to help girls complete high school in countries such as Ethiopia, Guatemala, and Nepal.

She's the First uses social media to inspire high school and college students in the United States to sponsor a girl in another country. Interested students form a "chapter" in their school or college. She's the First matches each chapter with a girl who needs money to go to school. It provides each chapter with encouragement and guidance in its fundraising.

Chapters can raise funds however they like. Many rely on money generated through events like bake sales. After the fundraising is done, She's the First makes sure that the sponsored girl receives the scholarship. It also updates the chapter on the sponsored girl's progress. She's the First now has 193 chapters supporting girls in 11 countries.

Members of a She's the First chapter generate donations to send girls to school in other communities (right). For example, some chapters have held bake sales, where a favorite sale item was "tie dye" cupcakes (below). Bake sale profits become donations.

Employing People

The waitstaff at O.NOIR in Toronto are all visually impaired.

Sometimes, the strategy of employing people is the simplest solution to a social problem. Employment provides skills training, work experience, or economic opportunity to a particular group. In The Empowerment Plan example, the company helps homeless people by employing them.

Working in the Dark

In 1999, Jorge Spielmann launched the Blind Cow Restaurant in Switzerland. It serves all its guests in the dark. This is challenging for people who can see.

Of course, a person with visual impairments is the best qualified to guide them through this experience.

Being visually impaired often makes it hard for people to find a job. Spielmann employs waitstaff who are blind, which creates unique job opportunities for a whole group of people. Similar restaurants appeared in Paris, London, New York, and Montreal. Mohand Touat found his first job at the age of 46 as a waiter in *Dans le Noir* (In the Dark) in Paris. Along sidewalks and in street crossings, he finds his way with a cane. Inside the restaurant, Touat moves quickly and confidently. He helps sighted diners feel comfortable and find what they need. He says, "In the dark, we're the ones serving as guides, so we're sort of switching roles. I feel good here."

Employment for a Community

Some people may not call themselves social entrepreneurs although they have the same goals and driven personalities. Clarence Louie is chief of the Osoyoos Indian Band in British Columbia. He is driving the economic revival of his community by building businesses.

Chief Louie set up a corporation dedicated to encouraging business development within his community. The 400-member band now owns and runs multiple businesses. These include a vineyard, golf course, campground, gas and convenience store, gravel and concrete operation, cultural center, and the elegant Nk'Mip Resort.

Louie is driven by a desire to help his people. In his view, the band's businesses provide long-term jobs for band members. Beyond generating income for the community, he says this also gives people "a reason to get out of bed in the morning."

❚❚ It's all about having a purpose in life. . . . If you get people working, most of the social problems in a community fade away. ❚❚

— Clarence Louie, Chief, Osoyoos Indian Band

Chief Clarence Louie is legendary for his ability to focus on a goal.

Providing Goods and Services

Not-for-profit and for-profit enterprises alike sell goods and services to customers. In some cases, those goods and services themselves help make a change. In The Empowerment Plan example, they provide homeless people with sleeping-bag coats. The coats themselves have a social impact.

Not Just for Grown-Ups

Adults are not the only ones who can join the social entrepreneurship game. Many students run fundraisers for one cause or another. Some of them donate money or time to help people in need. Once in a while these efforts blossom into full-blown enterprises.

Katie's Krops started out small, with a cabbage seedling. Nine-year-old Katie Stagliano planted it in her backyard in Summerville, South Carolina. That cabbage grew to weigh an incredible 40 pounds (18 kg). When it was ready to be harvested, Stagliano's father suggested that she might want to donate it to a local soup kitchen. Serving her cabbage to the 275 guests was a life-changing experience. Stagliano wondered how many people an entire garden could feed, if a single cabbage could feed that many people.

With the help of her parents and school, Stagliano started a garden on the school grounds. The students helped maintain the garden, which was the size of a football field. All the produce went to lower-income families. After the first garden was a success, Katie's Krops expanded. Now it helps schoolchildren start their own school gardens. Eight years later, there were 83 Katie's Krops gardens in the United States, all growing a product—fresh vegetables—that helped to address the social problem of hunger in local communities. Katie's goal is to help start 500 gardens in 50 states.

❚❚ Growing vegetables is fun, and it is so great to help people. If I can do it, anyone can. It doesn't take a huge garden; just a pot on your front porch with one vegetable plant can make a difference. ❚❚

—Katie Stagliano, Founder, Katie's Krops

Could your school start a garden to help feed the hungry?

We know that the number of social enterprises is growing. So is the number of social entrepreneur networks—the communities that social entrepreneurs form to support one another. If the trend in the graph below continues, we can expect to see a lot more brilliant plans for making the world a better place.

Number of Social Entrepreneur Networks in the World

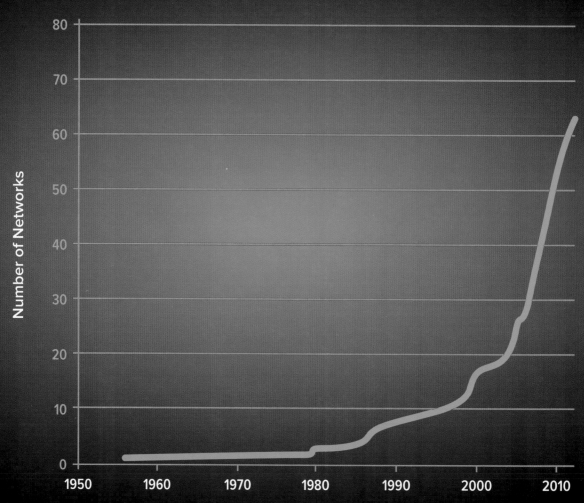

Social entrepreneurship networks in the world, compiled by Convergence 2015

More Opportunities

Worldwide, an economic downturn and advances in technology have caused an increasing loss of jobs. As a result, many young people today have a hard time finding secure, long-term employment. To meet this challenge, many are studying social entrepreneurship in college and university. Increasing numbers of young people may have the skills and initiative to create their own jobs through social enterprises.

Problems as Inspiration

Social entrepreneurship follows trends in social problems. For example, the world population continues to grow every year. This creates problems related to sanitation, unemployment, and other issues. As these problems become more pressing, social entrepreneurs will focus their efforts on solutions to those problems.

The News as Inspiration

Social entrepreneurs may get ideas from current events and social media. In 2015, for example, Syrians were fleeing the civil war in their country. Other countries were accepting few of these refugees, and their number kept growing until it became a crisis. The world paid little attention until a photo of a drowned refugee boy appeared in media around the world. The heartbreaking photo managed to put a face to the human crisis. Many countries began to respond, taking in refugees. In Germany, for example, social entrepreneurs also created enterprises that offered refugees housing, German lessons, and career coaching.

Building on Solutions

When social entrepreneurs succeed, others take their **innovative** solutions and adapt them to achieve different social goals or to address the same goal in different places. That means future social entrepreneurship will be shaped, in part, by which social enterprises succeed and how they do it.

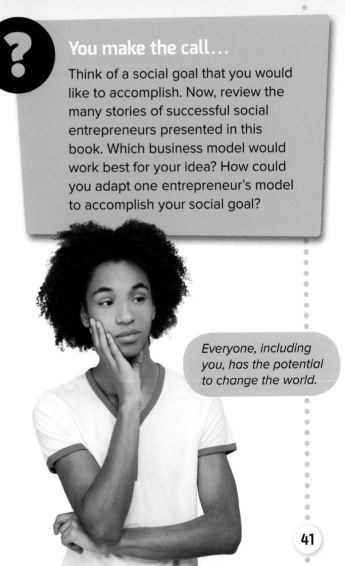

? You make the call...

Think of a social goal that you would like to accomplish. Now, review the many stories of successful social entrepreneurs presented in this book. Which business model would work best for your idea? How could you adapt one entrepreneur's model to accomplish your social goal?

Everyone, including you, has the potential to change the world.

The World Is Your Business

You can be someone who envisions a better future and makes it happen. And you can start right now! Maybe you've already learned some entrepreneurial skills. Perhaps you've stood up to a bully or run a food drive. Taking one small action may give you the confidence to tackle another, bigger challenge. And if you make mistakes, you learn how to do better next time. Either way, you and the people around you all benefit!

> ❚❚ It's really important for young people to start making a difference as early as they can. Youth can really have a tremendous impact. It's all about cultivating all of that positive energy toward something good. ❚❚
>
> – Yash Gupta, Founder, Sight Learning

Yash Gupta: Founder, Sight Learning

Yash Gupta started wearing glasses at the age of five. One day, he broke them in a martial arts class. He had to wait a week for new glasses. Without them, Gupta couldn't even see the whiteboard in class. He thought about the many children in the world who cannot afford glasses.

Gupta knew that people often throw away old glasses when they get new ones. He wondered if there was a way to get these to children who needed glasses.

Gupta made flyers and a website. He convinced a local pharmacy to host a drop-off box. He soon had 150 pairs of glasses to give away. By 2016, his enterprise, Sight Learning, had given away 26,000 pairs of glasses!

Yash Gupta was honored with a Nickelodeon Halo Award in 2014. This award honors teens who make a difference.

Think About It

1. What qualities do you have that would make you a good entrepreneur? Are you creative, driven, adaptable, idealistic, confident, independent, a team player, resourceful, or bold?

2. What qualities do you have that would make you a good social entrepreneur? Are you ethical, empathetic, optimistic, or visionary? Are you bothered by injustice? Do you have a sense of fairness?

3. What skills do you have that would make you a good social entrepreneur? Can you solve problems, spot opportunities, plan ahead, develop new ideas, or pay attention to details? Can you try something new, deal with setbacks, listen to others, focus on a goal, or put someone else before yourself?

4. In which of your communities do you see serious social problems? Consider your school, neighborhood, religious community, ethnic community, country, and world community.

5. Which social problems could you see yourself becoming passionate about? Consider poverty, illiteracy, racism, hunger, bullying, and childhood obesity.

6. Pick one social problem that needs a new answer. Now imagine that there are no barriers to your success: you are a super social entrepreneur! What cool enterprise could you put together to make the world a better place?

Next Steps

You too can become one of those remarkable people who start social enterprises. Investigate the social problems that you feel passionate about. What solutions have been tried, and why aren't they working? How could you do things differently? Discuss your best idea with your teachers, friends, and family. Figure out how you could make your vision a reality. Learn what skills and education you'll need. Above all, don't be afraid to take that first step. It could take you on an adventure that will change your life—and the lives of others!

Bibliography / Sources

Books

Bornstein, David. *How to Change the World: Social Entrepreneurs and the Power of New Ideas*. Oxford University Press, 2007.

Bornstein, David, and Susan Davis. *Social Entrepreneurship: What Everyone Needs to Know*. Oxford University Press, 2010.

Branson, Richard. *Screw Business as Usual*. The Penguin Group, 2011.

Chouinard, Yvon. *Let My People Go Surfing: The Education of a Reluctant Businessman*. The Penguin Group, 2005, 2006.

Frankl, Victor E. *Man's Search for Meaning*. Beacon Press, 1959, 2014.

Martin, Roger L., and Sally R. Osberg. *Getting Beyond Better: How Social Entrepreneurship Works*. Harvard Business Review Press, 2015.

Mycoskie, Blake. *Start Something that Matters*. Spiegel & Grau, 2011.

Thompson, Laurie Ann. *Be a Changemaker: How to Start Something that Matters*. Simon Pulse, 2014.

Websites

The Skoll Foundation. International organization that networks and supports social entrepreneurship.
http://skoll.org/

Ashoka: Innovators for the Public. A social entrepreneurship intern program.
www.ashoka.org/

Blended Value. High-level discussion of the value of business organizations and the purpose of capital.
www.blendedvalue.org/

ME to WE: An organization dedicated to helping people change the world.
www.metowe.com/about-us/our-organization/social-enterprise-an-innovative-new-model/

Social Enterprise Canada.
A national network for building social enterprise
www.socialenterprisecanada.ca/en

Articles

Abu-Saifan, Samer. "Social Entrepreneurship: Definitions and Boundaries." *Technology Innovation Management Review* (February 2012): 22–27.

Dees, J. Gregory. "The Meaning of 'Social Entrepreneurship.'" Original: October 31, 1998. Revised: May 30, 2001. https://entrepreneurship.duke.edu/news-item/the-meaning-of-social-entrepreneurship/

Kielburger, Craig and Marc. "Will Canada Lead in Fostering Social Entrepreneurship?" The Blog. *Huffington Post*. April 23, 2013. http://www.huffingtonpost.ca/craig-and-marc-kielburger/canada-social-entrepreurship_b_3141402.html

Martin, Roger L., and Sally Osberg. "Social Entrepreneurship: The Case for Definition." *Stanford Social Innovation Review* (Spring 2007). ssir.org/articles/entry/social_entrepreneurship_the_case_for_definition

Spence, Rick. "What It Really Means to Be a Social Entrepreneur." *Financial Post*. (September 15, 2015). http://business.financialpost.com/entrepreneur/fp-startups/what-it-really-means-to-be-a-social-entrepreneur?__lsa=18ab-2917

Learning More

Books to Read

Andrews, Carolyn. *What Are Goods and Services?* (Economics in Action). Crabtree Publishing, 2008.

Girard Golomb, Kristen. *Economics and You, Grades 5–8*. Mark Twain Media, 2012.

Hyde, Natalie. *What Is Entrepreneurship?* (Your Start-Up Starts Now!). Crabtree Publishing, 2016.

Mason, Helen. *What Is Digital Entrepreneurship?* (Your Start-Up Starts Now!). Crabtree Publishing, 2016.

Mycoskie, Blake. *Start Something That Matters*. Spiegel & Grau, 2011.

Offord, Alexander. *What Is Environmental Entrepreneurship?* (Your Start-Up Starts Now!). Crabtree Publishing, 2016.

Thompson, Laurie Ann. *Be a Changemaker: How to Start Something that Matters*. Simon Pulse, 2014.

Videos to Watch

Introduction to Social Entrepreneurship
www.teachertube.com/video/social-entrepreneurship-295387

Changing the World through Social Entrepreneurship: Willemijn Verloop at TEDxUtrecht.
http://tedxtalks.ted.com/search/?search=Willemijn+Verloop+at+TEDxUtrecht

Young Entrepreneur: Taybear. BizKids video.
http://bizkids.com/clip/profile-taybear.

Glossary

assembly line A method for creating products, whereby a product moves through a series of workers or machines, each with a specific task

business plan Planning document that includes all aspects of a business; used to assess whether a business will work and to get financing

charity A not-for-profit enterprise that provides social support or works for social change

digital entrepreneurship The activity of setting up new enterprises that use online or other electronic media for all or part of the business

donations Money given with the expectation of a social return

donors People who give money to not-for-profit social enterprises with the expectation of a social return

entrepreneur Person who starts a business based on their idea

entrepreneurship The process of turning an idea into a business

environmental entrepreneurship The activity of setting up new enterprises with the goal of making a positive impact on the environment

expenses The costs of producing goods and services, and the costs of running a business, such as rent and wages

for-profit Relating to a business that operates for the purpose of making money

goods Useful, physical items

grants Sums of money given by an organization to be used for a specified purpose; grants have no requirement to be repaid

injustice Lack of fairness

innovative Describing something or someone that uses ideas or methods

interest Money paid regularly at a certain rate as a fee for the use of money borrowed, or for delaying the repayment of a debt

investment Money given with the expectation of a financial return

investors People who give money to for-profit businesses with the expectation of a financial return

literacy The ability to read and write

loans Money given with the expectation of repayment and payment of a fee

logo A symbol used in advertising that identifies a company

marketing Advertising and promoting a product or service

market research The process of gathering information about consumer preferences

mentoring Training or advice from a trusted person with experience in a company, school, or type of business

microcredit Tiny loans given to people who normally would not qualify for a bank loan

not-for-profit Relating to an enterprise that does not operate for the purpose of making money

pilot project A small-scale practice run, with the goal to test an idea, and improve a design or approach

pitch A clear and exciting explanation of a business plan, used in an effort to get investors

profits Amount of money left over after a company's expenses have been subtracted from its total revenue

racism A belief that one race of people is superior to another

return on investment The payback that an investor receives, in the form of either money or social impact

revenue Money earned from sales

sanitation Conditions related to public health, especially access to clean drinking water and the safe disposal of human waste

services Work that is done for others

social entrepreneurship The activity of setting up new enterprises with the goal of positive social impact, that is, an improvement in people's lives

start-up (*n*) a new business; (*adj*) relating to the starting of a new business

start-up costs Money needed to cover the expenses of starting up a new business

taxes A required contribution to state revenue, set by the government on individuals' income, business profits, and property, and/or added to the cost of goods and services

venture A business enterprise involving some risk

Index

Author Biography

An educational writer and editor, Margaret Hoogeveen specializes in history, geography, social studies, and language arts. She holds both a Bachelor of English and a Bachelor of Education. In the course of her 25-year career, Margaret has created multiple classroom and teacher resources. She says that the best part about running her own business is the independence it gives her.